This book is dedicated to Scotty Wentzell.
His smile is infectious, he is brave, he inspires
many people, and he is kind and loving.
He brings so much joy to everyone he meets,
and the world is a better place with him in it.

— L.W., H.B., and C.D.

MCSEA BOOKS

A DOG & HIS BOY - The Adventures of Spillway & Scotty
Text © 2023 Heidi Bullen, Lisa Wentzell
Illustrations © 2023 Claudia Diller
All rights reserved.
Published in the United States of America by McSea Books, 2023
Manufactured by Regent Publishing Services Ltd. Printed in Shenzhen, China

McSea Books   Lincoln, Maine
www.mcseabooks.com

Cataloging-in-Publication Data has been applied for and may be obtained from the Library of Congress.

The Special Olympics logo and the name "Special Olympics" is reproduced with the kind permission of Special Olympics, Inc., Washington, DC [www.specialolympics.org], whose mission is to provide year-round sports training and athletic competition in a variety of Olympic-type sports for children and adults with intellectual disabilities, giving them continuing opportunities to develop physical fitness, demonstrate courage, experience joy and participate in a sharing of gifts, skills and friendship with their families, other Special Olympics athletes and the community.

ISBN: 9781954277144
Library of Congress Control Number: 2022919967

A DOG & HIS BOY

The Adventures of Spillway & Scotty

BY HEIDI BULLEN & LISA WENTZELL

ILLUSTRATED BY CLAUDIA DILLER

This is a story about
A dog and a boy,
And although I am stuffed,
I am not just a toy.

My name is Spillway,
I stay by my boy's side.
Wherever he goes,
I will happily guide.

My boy's name is Scotty,
We'll never part ways.
It'll be me and Scotty
For all of our days.

Born with a syndrome affecting his heart,
My Scotty was perfect, right from the start.

He was only a baby— just a few months old,
Developmental delays, is what we were told.

Together we have had some scary times.
But doctors and nurses made everything fine.

The way Scotty sees the world
Is not like me and you.
My Scotty sees the beauty
And all that's pure and true.

We share a special bond,
Neither one of us can talk.
And some things take more time,
Like learning how to walk.

My Scotty uses pictures to show us how he feels.
The things he wants and ones he loves,
His favorite places and meals.

Now, let me take you through
Our very busy year.
Adventures fill our days
And bring us lots of cheer.

Each year we go to Florida,
We'll spend time in the sun.
The beach waves crash right over us.
Oh, it's so much fun!

Always stoked to ride the waves
On Special Surfer Night.
Our dear friends help to guide us,
What an amazing sight!

Our happy place is camp,
It's wonderful and great,
We ride on boats and golf carts,
And even stay up late!

It's a blast at Pine Tree Camp
Where we spend time outside.
Hang in the treehouse, take a dip,
As nature and fun collide!

The lighthouse at Portland Head
Is Scotty's favorite spot!
We take in sights, breathe sea air,
And walk around a lot.

When we go riding horses,
He brings me right along.
Together we will hold on,
My Scotty's brave and strong.

Scotty rides his special bike
While we wave to our friends.
We cool off in the sprinkler—
And hope summer never ends.

Even a motorcycle club
Invited us to their crew.
Presented Scotty with a vest—
He proudly wears it too!

When the holidays come,
Sweet memories are made,

Hearts, shamrocks, bunnies,
Christmas trees, and parades.

Halloween is always fun —
With costumes for us too.
Super Scotty and Spillway
Are hiding, watch out!

BOO!

It's lots of fun to dress like chefs
When we cook and bake.
Our hats and aprons catch the splatters
And the spills we make.

A cake and birthday bash
At the firehouse to boot.
We even sit in the truck,
It surely is a hoot!

Wintertime is always filled
With skiing and with snow.
I'm sure to come along with him
Wherever he might go.

At Special Olympics, Scotty and I
Compete and do our best.
Both Mom and Dad will help us,
And then it's time to rest!

We see Scotty's friends at school,
He always makes them smile.
He loves to give a fist bump,
Because that's just his style.

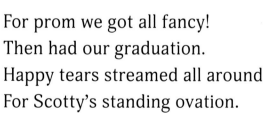

For prom we got all fancy!
Then had our graduation.
Happy tears streamed all around
For Scotty's standing ovation.

YAY!
SCOTTY
and
SPILLWAY!
HOORAY!
CONGRATS!

I'm with my very best friend
For most of every day.
But right before we go to sleep
We party and we play.

When it's time for him to rest,
I'll sit outside his door,
Waiting very patiently
Until I hear him snore.

Then I go in and snuggle up
Beside him nice and tight.
And we will snooze together
For the rest of the whole night.

Our adventures are great
And filled with such joy.
A life that's well-lived
For a dog and his boy.

Dear Reader:

My boy spreads love and kindness
Each and every day.
With smiles, hugs, and laughter—
In his special way.

See, Scotty is just like you
In so many different ways.
He loves making brand new friends
Throughout all of his days.

Even though it may be hard
Because he doesn't talk,
It really means a lot to him
To just go for a walk.

I truly treasure all the love
And everything we share.
It also means so much to us
When others show they care.

This life may often take a turn—
A different path than planned.
But this one's our perfect life,
It's wonderful and grand!

So, next time try and say hello
To those different from you.
Not only will you make them smile,
You'll find you're smiling too.

-Spillway

Thank You!

Special thanks go to these awesome organizations who have made so many of Spillway and Scotty's adventures possible!

Equip for Living
www.equipforliving.org

Maine Adaptive Sports & Recreation
www.maineadaptive.org

Special Olympics
www.specialolympics.org

Best Buddies Maine
www.bestbuddies.org

Riding to the Top Therapeutic Riding Center
www.ridingtothetop.org

Pine Tree Camp
www.pinetreesociety.org

Portland Wheelers
www.portlandwheelers.org

Special Surfers
www.specialsurfer.org

Meet the Creators

Heidi Bullen is a National Board Certified third-grade teacher at Crescent Park Elementary School in Bethel, Maine. She has been a teacher for twenty-four years. She lives in the mountains of Maine with her husband and two dogs and cherishes visits from her grown son and daughter. This is her third book.

Lisa Krikorian Wentzell is a full-time mom with a full-time career caring for Scotty, her special-needs son. Together with her husband, Scott, they are dedicated to assuring Scotty enjoys all that life has to offer. Everyone's life journey is different, and although their family journey is challenging, Lisa triumphs in uncovering hidden joys. She feels blessed with loving and supportive family, friends, teachers, and community, and with amazing programs that allow Scotty to downhill ski, ride horses, and surf. Lisa's empowering message in *A Dog and His Boy* is inclusion for children like Scotty.

Claudia Diller has lived in Maine for over fifty years and currently resides in Kingfield, where she writes and illustrates a weekly blog and paints her annual art calendar and note cards. She has written and illustrated one book and illustrated four others.